W9-CTX-972

EXTREME WEATHER

WEATHER AND CLIMATE

EXTREME WEATHER

Terry Jennings

A+
Smart Apple Media

First published in 2005 by Evans Brothers Limited
2A Portman Mansions, Chiltern Street
London W1U 6NR

Designer: Giraffic Design, Editor: Mary-Jane Wilkins, Illustrator:
Graham Rosewarne, Series consultant: Steve Watts

Picture acknowledgements
Corbis: page 2, 6 (top), 9 (bottom), 11 (bottom), 15, 17, 25, 29
Ecoscene: page 9 (top), 20, 35 (top), 38 (top), 43 (bottom)
Terry Jennings: page 10, 11 (top), 30 (bottom), 32, 34, 43 (top)
Oxford Scientific: front cover, page 6 (bottom), 7, 12, 16, 21, 26,
37 (bottom), 40
Still Pictures: page 14. 18, 19, 22, 23 (top and bottom), 24, 27,
28, 30 (top), 31, 33, 35 (bottom), 36, 37 (top), 39, 41, 42, 45

Published in the United States by Smart Apple Media
2140 Howard Drive West, North Mankato, Minnesota 56003

Library of Congress Cataloging-in-Publication Data

Jennings, Terry J.
Extreme weather / by Terry Jennings.
p. cm. — (Weather and climate)
Includes index.
ISBN 1-58340-727-8
1. Storms—Juvenile literature.
2. Droughts—Juvenile literature. I. Title.

QC941.3.J46 2005
551.55—dc22   2004066424

9 8 7 6 5 4 3 2 1

Contents

Weather and atmosphere

Today, floods, droughts, tornadoes, hurricanes, and other weather disasters wreck people's lives all over the world, despite advances in technology. To understand the causes of extreme weather, we first need to know about the causes of more typical weather.

The ruins of a building battered by Hurricane Charley when it struck Florida in August 2004.

The peaks of the Chugach Mountains in Alaska are covered in snow year-round because of their height and latitude.

The air around us
We live at the bottom of a sea of air called the atmosphere. It provides the air we breathe and insulates Earth. It acts as a sunshade during the day, protecting us from excessive heat, and as a blanket at night, preventing Earth from cooling too much. It filters out radiation from the sun and makes meteorites burn up by friction before they hit Earth. Nine-tenths of the atmosphere is in the layer from the ground up to about 10 miles (16 km) above Earth.

The layers of the atmosphere
The air surrounding Earth has three main layers. The lowest, the troposphere, stretches up to about 10 miles (16 km) and contains 90 percent of the mass of the air. The temperature here falls rapidly with increasing height, and at its upper limit is about -76 °F (-60 °C). Most storms begin in the troposphere, and great moving masses of air keep the clouds in motion. The stratosphere, the second main layer, reaches up to about 50 miles (80 km). It has low concentrations of the atmospheric gases. Above is a belt in which the gases are even thinner and their atoms are electrically charged, or ionized, by the sun's radiation.

Air pressure and temperature

Although it is invisible, air has substance and consists of atoms and molecules in the same way as liquids and solids. Air also has weight, and 35 cubic feet (1 cu m) weighs about 2.76 pounds (1.25 kg). Because of this, air exerts a pressure on all the surfaces it touches. This is greatest at sea level, where it is equivalent to about 13 pounds (6 kg) on 1 square inch (6 sq cm). The higher you go, the lower the pressure becomes.

Air pressure varies, and these changes can be recorded with a barometer and used to forecast weather in temperate (or middle) latitudes (those with neither very hot nor very cold climates). High pressure usually means fair weather, and when the barometer falls, it is likely to rain. Temperatures on Earth vary from place to place and are affected by altitude, latitude, land and sea, wind, ocean currents, clouds, and relief.

The sun doesn't heat air directly. Instead, the sun's rays heat Earth's surface, which radiates back the heat that warms the air. You feel a drop in temperature if you climb a mountain and move away from the source of the heat, Earth's surface. The drop averages 3.6 °F (2 °C) per 1,000 feet (300 m).

Temperature and latitude

Temperature also gradually drops the farther away from the equator you go. This is why there is permanent snow and ice in the polar regions, yet high temperatures in the tropics. These differences are caused by the fact that the sun's rays strike the area away from the equator with less warming power than at the equator itself. Also, to reach Earth's surface, the sun's rays pass through the atmosphere,

WEATHER MACHINE

The atmosphere is like a vast machine. The energy that drives the machine comes from the sun, and it is also fueled by air and water. The power the machine produces is shown as various types of weather, including winds, rainstorms, snowstorms, and thunderstorms.

The weather on this island in French Polynesia is influenced by its distance from the equator, as well as by the Pacific Ocean, which surrounds it.

atmosphere

→
sun's rays

→
sun's rays

where much of their heat is reflected back by clouds and dust. The rays have to travel farther to reach the poles than the equator. The farther they travel, the more heat they lose. This explains seasonal variations in temperature. Clouds reduce the sun's warming effect, causing variations in temperature.

THE EFFECT OF EARTH'S CURVATURE ON THE SUN'S RAYS

Land and sea

As the sun's rays strike Earth, they are absorbed by a very thin layer of Earth's crust. By contrast, over the sea, the rays penetrate deeply, and their heating power spreads farther. The sea has to absorb more solar radiation than the land for its temperature to be raised by the same amount. On a sunny day, the land is much hotter than the sea. The land also loses heat more quickly and cools down as fast as it warms up. So land surfaces can have great ranges of temperature between night and day and from season to season. The opposite is true of the sea.

Wind and ocean currents

Like the air of the atmosphere, the waters of the oceans mix and circulate. Warm water from the tropics flows toward the poles, and cold water from the polar regions flows toward the equator. These currents may form a definite stream, such as the Gulf Stream, or they may slow down and spread out to form drifts. Winds blowing over warm ocean currents are warmed. Warm air holds more water than cold, and warm winds blowing across the ocean pick up moisture from the surface. When they reach land, they bring rain. Winds blowing over cold ocean currents to land are cooled. They do not hold much moisture and dry the land they pass over.

THE WORLD'S OCEAN CURRENTS

Winds blowing over warm ocean currents are warmed, while those blowing over cold currents are cooled. Water takes between 500 and 2,000 years to make one complete trip around the world.

Warm currents
Cold currents

Cloud barriers

Clouds act as barriers to the sun's radiation. The world's highest temperatures are recorded under the clear, sunny skies of tropical deserts. Clouds also check the heat radiated by Earth, so cloudy areas tend to have a small daily range of temperature, compared with the hot days and cold nights of tropical deserts.

The shape of the land

The shape, or relief, of the land surface causes temperature variations. Vineyards and orchards are planted on the sides of valleys because heavy, cold air moves down slopes, and pockets of freezing air may lie in the valley bottom. Mountain villages in the Alps grew up on the north side of valleys because they receive more of the sun's radiation there. Mountains can also restrict the circulation of air in the lower atmosphere. The Rockies restrict the penetration of warm, moist air from the Pacific Ocean, so the interior of North America has more extreme continental weather conditions.

Winds and pressure belts

The air of the lower atmosphere moves constantly, forming winds. The propelling force for this is heat energy from the sun. As air is warmed, it expands and rises, forming low pressure areas. And as the warmer, lighter air rises, masses of denser, cooler air move in as wind to take its place. On Earth, the heat of the tropics acts like a radiator heating the air. This warm air is less dense, which makes it rise so that cooler air is drawn in from elsewhere to take its place. As a result, most winds that blow over Earth move from the cold poles toward the equator.

The rotation of Earth swings the masses of air around faster at the equator than at the poles, so the winds in the northern hemisphere are deflected to the east, and those in the southern hemisphere to the west. As the winds blow, local forces can override global ones. Land masses warm and cool more quickly than the sea, so new high and low pressure areas form at different times of the day in different seasons.

The Negev Desert in Israel. Temperatures are highest under the clear, sunny skies of tropical deserts like this.

High winds bend a tree photographed from inside the eye of a hurricane in Florida.

Cumulonimbus clouds loom over Lisbon, Portugal. These towering clouds bring heavy rain and thunderstorms.

Water vapor in the air

The water vapor in the atmosphere is a gas, and the amount in the air depends on the temperature. The higher the temperature, the more water vapor the air can hold. When air is holding the maximum amount, it is saturated. Usually, it is less than saturated, and the amount of water vapor is recorded as a percentage of the total possible, called relative humidity. Most air does not have to be cooled much before it becomes saturated. If the air is cooled further, it can no longer hold the water vapor, and it condenses into water droplets.

Millions of tons of water are carried in the atmosphere as invisible water vapor or clouds. Warm air carries more moisture than cold, so when warm air is cooled, it can no longer retain its water vapor. As it condenses around the tiny particles of dust, salt, pollen, or plant spores in the air, it forms microscopic water droplets, which form clouds.

There are three main types of clouds. Cirrus clouds are made of ice crystals at high altitudes (above 19,680 feet [6,000 m]) and appear as thin, feathery streaks. Cumulus clouds are thick with a flat base and domes or billows above. Their bases are below 6,600 feet (2,000 m). Stratus is a layer of clouds with a base between the ground and 6,600 feet (2,000 m), which may be hundreds of feet thick and bring drizzle or rain. Some clouds are mixtures of two types.

Rain, thunder, and lightning

In temperate regions, rain starts at the top of clouds as ice crystals. Some melt and fall as rain and some freeze again after melting and become sleet or snow. In the polar regions, cold air carries little moisture, so clouds are rare, and there is little rain or snow. In the tropics, heavy rain falls most days. When rising warm moisture builds into thunderclouds, they become electrically charged. As the electricity discharges from one cloud to another, or from a cloud to Earth, the current heats the surrounding air to white heat—a lightning flash. Instantly, the air expands and causes the sound waves of a thunderclap.

MEASURING CLOUD COVER

Meteorologists record cloud cover—the extent to which clouds cover the sky. It is usually measured in oktas. This is a scale of 1 to 8. A sky with 8 oktas is completely covered, and a sky with 0 oktas is cloudless.

Snow and fog

At 19,680 feet (6,000 m) and above, clouds are composed of ice crystals suspended in the air until they combine into snowflakes large enough to fall. They are six-sided, and no two are exactly alike. Many melt as they pass through warmer air on their way down, and they reach the ground as sleet or rain.

Fog is produced when the air is saturated. As it cools, the water vapor condenses into droplets of water too small and light to fall. Fog is really a cloud at ground level. It may form when the ground cools at night and chills the damp air above it, or when warm, moist air moves over a cold ocean current or cool land area.

Fog forming over farmland in Norfolk, England, as the ground begins to cool at the end of the day.

This satellite photograph shows a hurricane approaching the Gulf Coast of the United States. Satellites help forecasters to predict accurately where and when a hurricane will hit land.

Hurricanes

2

Hurricanes bring destructive winds, severe thunderstorms, vast quantities of rain, and waterspouts. They force seawater into devastating waves. They are the largest storms on Earth.

Hurricane Georges whips up the sea and pulls at palm trees as it approaches Florida in 1998.

How hurricanes are formed

Every year, about 60 huge storms that generate speeds of more than 75 miles (120 km) per hour develop over tropical oceans. The meteorological name for these storms is tropical cyclone. In the west Pacific, north of the equator, strong tropical cyclones are called typhoons. In the Indian Ocean and the southwest Pacific Ocean, they are known as cyclones. When they form over the Atlantic or eastern Pacific, they are called hurricanes. In Australia, these violent storms are called willy-willies.

Most hurricanes form within the doldrums, a narrow tropical belt between the northeast and southeast trade winds, where the temperature is greater than 75 °F (24 °C). The doldrums of the Atlantic are mainly north of the equator, so the south Atlantic Ocean does not have hurricanes. By contrast, the Pacific doldrums extend both north and south of the equator, so hurricanes occur in both of these regions.

A hurricane forms when moist air is warmer than the surface of the ocean. Denser, colder air pushes underneath this warm, saturated air. The atmospheric pressure within the rising warm air drops sharply, and the wind speed increases. The newly formed storm picks up vast amounts of energy and moisture as it rushes toward land. The heat and water vapor often create violent thunderstorms. These may group together if the water is above 75 °F (24 °C). They spin around as one large system, and as they are pushed farther across the ocean by the wind, they draw in more warm, moist air, gathering energy. They spin in ever-tighter circles, their speed increased by Earth's rotation. When the wind speed reaches 75 miles (120 km) per hour, the storm becomes a hurricane. Hurricanes can produce sustained wind speeds of 155 miles (250 km) per hour, with gusts up to 185 miles (300 km) per hour. Tornadoes produce stronger winds but are short-lived, whereas a hurricane can last for a week or two and cover thousands of miles.

The hurricane season

During the summer and autumn in the tropical regions, the ocean surface and the air above it are warm. High winds evaporate the sea water rapidly, and the water vapor rises to form clouds. Large amounts of heat are released into the atmosphere by condensation, and this provides the energy that fuels the system.

The structure of a hurricane

A hurricane can measure 250 miles (400 km) across. Inside, a swirling mass of winds spirals upward. At the center, or eye, of the storm, the skies are clear, and temperatures are high. The calm eye may be 25 miles (40 km) across, but the strongest winds are immediately around it. The storms with the smallest eye are often the most powerful. Around the eye are thick, swirling clouds that tower six miles (10 km) above sea level. As this warm, moist air spirals upward, the water vapor cools and turns to rain, releasing the hurricane's energy.

SWIRLING STORMS

Hurricanes turn counterclockwise in the northern hemisphere and clockwise in the southern hemisphere because of Earth's rotation.

INSIDE A HURRICANE

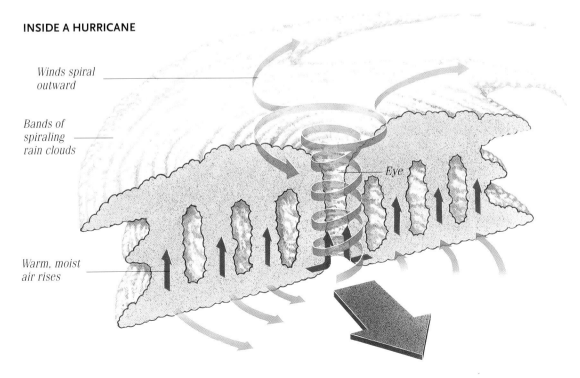

Winds spiral outward

Bands of spiraling rain clouds

Eye

Warm, moist air rises

Cars were wrecked, trees were uprooted, and buildings were reduced to rubble when Hurricane Mitch struck Honduras in the autumn of 1998.

A hurricane takes several days to travel from the ocean, where it was formed, to land. As it roars by, it may seem that the storm has ended as the eye passes overhead. The wind and heavy rain of the hurricane are followed by clear skies and an unnatural calm. Within an hour or two, however, the eye passes, and the other side of the hurricane hits, bringing more destructive winds and torrential rain.

Hurricane strengths

Every hurricane is classified according to its strength on a scale from 1 to 5. This helps people in its path know how strong it is going to be, and to decide whether to board up windows, seek the safety of a storm shelter, or evacuate the area. The mildest hurricane is a Category 1 and has wind speeds of at least 75 miles (120 km) per hour. The strongest and rarest is a Category 5, with wind speeds faster than 155 miles (250 km) per hour. These are the most feared hurricanes. Hurricane Andrew, a Category 5 hurricane in 1992, holds the record for being the most costly in American history. Hurricane Mitch, which hit Central America in autumn 1998, also reached Category 5. The most recent was Hurricane Ivan, which reached Category 5 over the Windward Islands in September 2004.

Enormous energy

Scientists estimate that a single hurricane can unleash more energy in a day than 500,000 atomic bombs.

Hurricanes follow a curved path. At first, they move west with the trade winds, but like all great air movements, they are deflected in their path by Earth's rotation. This is called the Coriolis effect. In the northern hemisphere, a hurricane usually follows a northwesterly path. In the higher latitudes, it then curves around toward the northeast. In the southern hemisphere, a hurricane usually begins traveling southwest and then veers around to the southeast. Near the equator, hurricane speeds vary from 5 to 20 miles (8–32 km) per hour, but in the higher latitudes it can be as much as 50 miles (80 km) per hour.

Hurricane damage

A hurricane can uproot trees and lift boats from harbors and fling them over harbor walls. Houses are destroyed as their roofs are torn off, and large trucks are lifted off the road. Cables and wires are ripped from their poles, and anyone outdoors stands little chance of survival.

The force of the hurricane also creates huge waves on the sea. The water level near or under a hurricane can be 16 feet (5 m) or more higher than the calmer seas around it. These waves are called a hurricane surge. When they reach land, they cause serious flooding. A hurricane surge may last only a few hours, but its crashing waves usually cause severe damage. Most deaths in a hurricane are from drowning.

Hurricane damage occurs mainly on islands and in coastal areas. The storm usually dies out fairly quickly once it is away from the ocean from which it takes its energy and moisture. The friction caused by the land also slows the winds, so they become less damaging.

Naming and studying hurricanes

Australian meteorologist Clement Wragge (1852–1922) was the first person to give hurricanes names. He chose the names of people from the Bible. Later, the United States Weather Bureau gave female names to hurricanes. Since 1978, meteorologists have drawn up a list of alternate boys' and girls' names, in alphabetical order. Every time a new hurricane is detected, it is given the next name on the list.

Meteorologists need to find out how hurricanes form so they can forecast them accurately, reduce the damage they cause, or even keep them from developing. Hurricanes are very difficult to study since they destroy scientific instruments and kill anyone who goes near them.

A satellite photograph showing both Hurricane Frances (top left corner) and Hurricane Ivan (bottom right corner) over the Caribbean in the summer of 2004.

Flying through a hurricane

A few specially strengthened military aircraft can fly through hurricanes to measure the wind speeds and directions, the location and size of the eye, and the air pressures and temperature changes within them. Scientists on board have reported that the heaviest rain falls in spiral bands. Inside the eye, the air is pure and clear, while the surrounding clouds rise up in tiers. The water vapor inside the clouds instantly turns to ice on the aircraft's wings. There is a dome of clear blue sky high above the hurricane. Other aircraft, called hurricane hunters, fly around the edges of hurricanes and track their position.

A satellite photograph of Hurricane Linda, which formed off the west coast of Mexico in September 1997.

The role of satellites

Satellites take photographs of storms as they grow. These help scientists predict when a hurricane is going to develop and its likely path. They also record changes in the temperature of the ocean surface as a hurricane forms in the atmosphere. Satellites track every low pressure area that might lead to a full-scale hurricane. They send data to monitoring centers, such as the National Hurricane Center in Florida.

Forecasting hurricanes

There are several warning signs when a hurricane is approaching. First come dull red sunsets caused by a thin haze of clouds. The air becomes very hot and humid, and the air pressure, as shown by a barometer, is high as the wind dies down. At sea, there is a growing swell. As the storm approaches, the barometer needle drops suddenly because the air pressure falls rapidly. A rain cloud rushes toward the land and torrential rain begins.

Injuries and deaths caused by hurricanes have been greatly reduced because of improved methods of forecasting. The hurricane that struck Galveston, Texas, in 1900 was the most deadly disaster ever to befall the United States. Reaching speeds of about 105 miles (170 km) per hour, the hurricane is believed to have killed 10,000 to 12,000 people. It caused an estimated $20 million in damage.

More recently, Hurricane Andrew, which blasted its way across the Bahamas, the Gulf of Mexico, southern Florida, and Louisiana in August 1992, caused damage estimated at $26.5 billion. Andrew was about 500 miles (800 km) in diameter, but its fiercest winds, around the eye, gusted up to 200 miles (320 km) per hour. In the four hours Andrew took to cross Florida, it destroyed 80,000 homes and damaged 55,000 more. It also destroyed 15,000 boats.

Television and radio broadcast alerts about Hurricane Andrew's approach allowed about a million people to flee north out of its path. Most of those who stayed went to a public hurricane shelter or were in concrete houses. So in spite of the record-breaking amount of damage Andrew caused, it killed fewer than 50 people.

A mobile home park destroyed by Hurricane Charley in Punta Gorda, Florida, in August 2004.

3

Tornadoes

Tornadoes are small, very powerful whirlwinds that form very suddenly. The word tornado comes from the Latin word *tornare,* meaning to twist or turn.

TORNADO DISASTERS

The swarm of tornadoes that struck the Madaripur district of Bangladesh in April 1977 killed almost 900 people and injured more than 6,000. Bangladesh was also the scene of the world's worst tornado disaster in 1989, in which 1,300 people died.

Where tornadoes occur

A tornado is smaller and faster than a hurricane, but it can be more destructive, destroying everything in its path. It appears as a twisting funnel cloud up to 650 feet (200 m) high, stretching down from a storm cloud to Earth. A tornado travels at up to 75 miles (120 km) per hour. Inside, the wind speed can reach 500 miles (800 km) per hour—the highest on Earth. It is impossible to be sure, because a tornado would destroy any wind-speed recorder. Tornadoes vary in size from 10 feet (3 m) across to more than 1,650 feet (500 m) and can travel 125 miles (200 km) per hour. They are strongest in the temperate latitudes where the effect of Earth's rotation is greatest. The most violent tornadoes occur in the U.S., which has about 1,000 a year. Tornadoes also occur in parts of Canada, Argentina, China, Australia, Southwest Asia, the Indian subcontinent, and even Europe. The United Kingdom has 15 to 30 small tornadoes a year.

A tornado over south central Kansas in May 2001. Tornadoes commonly occur in the Great Plains and the southeastern U.S.

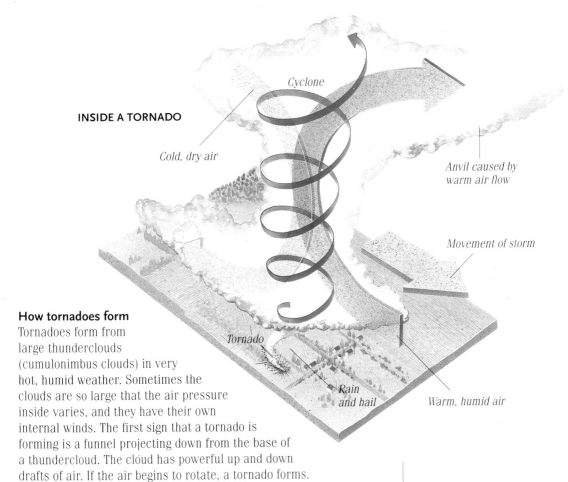

INSIDE A TORNADO

Cyclone

Cold, dry air

Anvil caused by warm air flow

Movement of storm

Tornado

Rain and hail

Warm, humid air

How tornadoes form

Tornadoes form from large thunderclouds (cumulonimbus clouds) in very hot, humid weather. Sometimes the clouds are so large that the air pressure inside varies, and they have their own internal winds. The first sign that a tornado is forming is a funnel projecting down from the base of a thundercloud. The cloud has powerful up and down drafts of air. If the air begins to rotate, a tornado forms.

There are about 45,000 thunderstorms a day around the world, yet few spawn tornadoes. Instead, they usually produce heavy rain, thunder, or hail. One sign of a forming tornado is dark patches of cloud, shaped like stubby fingers, hanging from the base of a thundercloud. These may grow until a funnel-shaped cloud hangs below the parent cloud. Many fade after about ten minutes, but sometimes the funnel grows. The cloud twists downward faster and faster, until the funnel reaches the ground. At first, the tornado is made up of tiny water droplets. But the moment the cloud touches the ground, it sucks up soil, sand, dust, and other debris. That is why a tornado appears black.

Changing air pressure

Much of the damage caused by a tornado comes from the sudden changes in air pressure it creates. At the center of the tornado, the air pressure is very low. This low pressure core acts as a powerful vacuum cleaner,

Damage caused by a tornado that struck Moore, Oklahoma. Neither cars nor homes are safe when a tornado strikes.

and tornadoes have been known to pick up trucks, horses, whole trees, and even people. Buildings in the path of a tornado are likely to be badly damaged. The pressure inside the houses and other buildings it passes over remains normal. As the tornado passes over, the sudden drop in outside pressure causes the air inside the buildings to expand violently, and the buildings explode like a popped balloon.

Tracking tornadoes

The relatively small size and brief life of tornadoes (two-thirds last less than three minutes) make them difficult to predict, but a kind of radar has increased the accuracy of tornado forecasts. Since 1977, Doppler radar has been used to detect the circular movements inside storms that can develop into tornadoes. The radar can predict a tornado about 25 minutes before it emerges from the base of the clouds. This allows just enough time to send out warnings. Better forecasting and communication is helping to save lives. Tornadoes killed about 100 people in the U.S. every year during the 1970s. By the 1990s, this had fallen to 50.

A waterspout whirls over the estuary of the River Humber in England. Waterspouts cause much less damage than tornadoes.

Waterspouts

Waterspouts are rapidly rotating columns of air that form over water—usually a lake or a sea. They resemble tornadoes over water. They are never as severe as a tornado funnel on land, and the average wind speeds in a waterspout are about 50 miles (80 km) per hour. However, waterspouts do not need severe thunderstorms to set them in motion. The visible funnel of the waterspout is caused by water droplets that have condensed from the air because of the low pressure inside the spiraling waterspout.

Waterspouts need warm water to develop and are common in the Florida Keys. They also happen in coastal regions of the equatorial Atlantic and Indian Oceans, the Mediterranean, and the Gulf of Mexico. Some are isolated, while others occur in clusters.

The first sign of a developing waterspout is often a shadow on the water where the rotating air is disturbing the surface. Once it has formed, the waterspout slowly follows a curved path. After about 15 minutes, cooler air enters the funnel of the waterspout, causing it to lose energy and disappear.

The highest waterspout recorded was seen in May 1898 off Eden in New South Wales, Australia. A reading taken with a theodolite from the shore showed it to be 5,012 feet (1,528 m) high and about 10 feet (3 m) wide. Waterspouts can be a hazard to small boats, and sometimes they cause injury and loss of life.

Dust devils

A dust devil is an upward-swirling mass of dust-filled air varying in height from a few feet to more than 1,000 feet (300 m). Unlike tornadoes, dust devils form from the ground up. When air near the ground becomes much warmer than the air above, it becomes unstable, begins to rise, and draws more air in underneath it, sucking up dust in the process.

Dust devils resemble miniature tornadoes but are very short-lived and much less damaging. They are common in hot, dry desert and semidesert regions of the world, particularly Africa. In the Sahara Desert, dust devils can last from a few minutes to a few hours, every day. In Tucson, Arizona, there are about 80 dust devils every day.

A dust devil is an upward-swirling mass of dust-filled air. Dust devils are common in hot, dry parts of the world.

Thunderstorms

Thunderstorms happen on hot days when moist air close to the ground is heated and rises quickly. They are common in many parts of the world, and in some parts of the tropics, thunderstorms occur most days during the rainy season.

LIGHTNING STRIKES

There is a saying that lightning never strikes the same place twice. But during one thunderstorm, the Empire State Building in New York was struck by lightning 15 times in 15 minutes.

Air currents

An updraft may start over ground that has been heated more strongly by the sun than the surrounding land. The rapidly rising air currents lead to the formation of towering cumulonimbus clouds with a characteristic anvil-shaped top. These thunderclouds may be only a few miles across and yet may tower 12 miles (20 km) into the sky.

Cloud to ground lightning photographed at night in Oklahoma. Only about one lightning flash in four travels from a cloud to the ground.

Inside a thundercloud, strong upward and downward air currents sweep ice crystals, ice pellets, and water droplets past and into each other. These movements create static electricity that builds up in the cloud. Positive electric charges collect toward the top of the cloud, and negative charges collect in the lower parts. They are strongly attracted to each other. Eventually, the layer of air between the charges cannot keep them apart any longer and a massive spark—lightning—is released as the charges neutralize themselves.

The lightning discharge is usually within a cloud, between clouds, or between a cloud and the air. Only about one in four lightning flashes travels from a cloud to the ground. Then the lightning is attracted to the higher parts of Earth's surface. This is why lightning conductors are placed on tall buildings and why it is dangerous to shelter under a tree in a thunderstorm. One of the safest places to be in a thunderstorm is inside a car, as the tires provide insulation.

Sprites

Until recently, aircraft were thought to be safe in a thunderstorm because they are not in contact with the ground and therefore cannot conduct electricity. But scientists recently discovered that lightning flashes, called sprites, are sometimes discharged from the top of a thundercloud toward space. These are suspected of causing a small number of aircraft crashes.

Two lightning bolts strike mountain foothills in Tucson, Arizona.

The sound of thunder

The temperature of a lightning flash is more than 40,000 °F (22,000 °C). It superheats the air around it, making it expand at an incredible speed and then contract equally rapidly. This creates the sound waves that we hear as thunder. Light travels faster than sound, so we see the lightning flash before we hear the thunder. The closer the thunderclap and lightning flash are to each other, the nearer the thunderstorm is.

Hailstones left after a thunderstorm. Large hailstones may contain many layers of ice, and they can cause great damage to crops, greenhouses, and cars.

Frozen hailstones

Because a thundercloud is so tall, its upper levels are well below the freezing point. The rising air currents inside the cloud vary in strength. A raindrop on a strong rising current may be swept so high that it freezes, only to fall again as the air current weakens. At lower levels, a frozen raindrop may collect more water, which freezes on the next upward thrust. This process may be repeated many times. Hailstones with 25 layers of ice have been recorded. They can do great damage to crops, greenhouses, and cars, and can injure people. The worst hail disaster on record struck India in 1888, when hailstones the size of baseballs battered Moradabad, killing 246 people. In tropical areas, hailstones are often formed in thunderclouds but rarely reach the ground because high temperatures melt them on the way down.

Floods

Floods can cause great damage and loss of life, although sometimes they can be useful. Flooding may be triggered when heavy rain or rapidly melting snow produces more water than a river can hold. Serious coastal flooding occurs when a strong wind blows toward the land during a high tide.

Why rivers flood

The most extreme flooding occurs in tropical regions, where seasonal winds called monsoons bring heavy rains. Many parts of the world have sudden, heavy rainstorms, especially places that receive most of their rain during one short, wet season. The rain swells the rivers and can flood land far away.

A river may also flood if it becomes blocked. The long rivers that flow north to the Arctic Ocean in northern Canada and Russia freeze over in winter. When spring comes, the ice melts in the warmer parts of the rivers farther south before it melts in the northern stretches near their mouths. The rivers fill up with the melted snow, but their mouths are still frozen. When the meltwater reaches the ice blockage, the rivers overflow and flood the land.

A girl wades through floods in Dhaka, the capital of Bangladesh. The city occupies a low-lying site on the Ganges delta and is flooded regularly.

THE COST OF FLOODS

Floods kill more people than any other weather disaster. They ruin the lives of millions more and cause billions of dollars worth of damage every year.

This aerial photograph shows the River Ganges snaking toward its delta over low-lying land.

Rocks and flooding

Some rocks, such as chalk and sandstone, are permeable and soak up water like a sponge. Other rocks, such as clay and granite, are impermeable, and they can help to make flooding worse because they don't let water through. The water runs over their surface and quickly fills up rivers and streams. Towns and cities have huge areas of blacktop and concrete, which act in the same way as impermeable rocks. Heavy rain runs off of these surfaces into drains, which flow into rivers and streams. The sudden rush of water can make the rivers and streams overflow and flood.

Useful floods

When a river nears the sea or a lake, it flows across flat lowland. Here the river flows along slowly in huge curves called meanders. This combination of flat land and wide meanders allows floodwater to spread out across a large area of land. This area is called a floodplain. When a river floods, water pours over its banks, dumping mud and sand over the land. These make a very fertile soil called alluvial soil.

Floods in Bangladesh

Most of the country of Bangladesh lies on a delta at the mouths of the Rivers Ganges and Brahmaputra. This flat floodplain is one of the largest in the world. The two great rivers often flood, leaving a layer of fertile mud over the plain. As long as the monsoon rains fall, up to three crops of rice are grown here in a year. However, in some years, the monsoon rains fail to arrive, and when this happens, there is a drought and food shortage.

In other years, the rains are very heavy, and the flooding is severe. Too much water destroys the crops and damages buildings, power supplies, and roads. In severe floods, many people die.

SEA LEVELS

Over the last 18,000 years, sea levels have risen by about 400 feet (120 m). At the end of the last Ice Age, the ice and snow that covered much of the land started to melt, flooding many low-lying coastal areas as the sea flowed inland, altering the shape of the coastline.

Flash floods

The most spectacular and rapid floods are flash floods. Most are caused when a thunderstorm or hurricane brings a short, heavy burst of rain over mountains. Then the water level in the mountain streams rises very quickly and sends a wall of water rushing as fast as an express train into the valley below. Other flash floods are caused by the rapid melting of snow or a burst dam.

Thunderstorm floods

Although few thunderstorms last more than an hour or two, in that time they can release more than 25 million gallons (100 million l) of water. This can cause huge, unexpected flooding.

In August 1996, a severe thunderstorm hit the Pyrennees Mountains in northern Spain. The sky darkened and hailstones the size of golf balls fell. They were followed by three inches (8 cm) of rain in two hours. The rain washed soil, stones, boulders, and trees into a mountain stream, which quickly became a raging torrent. Downstream, artificial drainage channels rapidly filled with water. Suddenly, a giant wall of water crashed down the valley and through a nearby campground. A total of 87 people died, and 180 were injured. Some bodies were found 10 miles (16 km) from the campground.

A flash flood caused by a thunderstorm over Death Valley in California.

Desert floods

In many hot desert areas, the sun bakes the ground hard like concrete. When there is a heavy rainstorm, the water rushes over the compacted surface, filling gullies and dry river beds in seconds. In the deserts of North America, more people drown in flash floods than die from thirst.

Bursting dams

Dam bursts are another major cause of flash flooding. A dam is a large wall or bank built to hold back the water in a river. A man-made lake, called a reservoir, fills up behind the dam. Dams are built across river valleys to store water for drinking, irrigating crops, and producing electricity. They can even help to stop flooding by holding back the water that would otherwise inundate areas farther downstream. But if a dam bursts, it can cause a devastating flood.

Temporary dams

Trees, rocks, and other debris washed away by heavy rain can become trapped by a bridge, forming a temporary dam. The water level rises behind the dam until the dam and bridge eventually burst under the pressure of the water, resulting in a flash flood.

Flood disasters

Slow-rising floods often cause the most deaths and greatest destruction, especially in Asia. In China, if the monsoon rains last longer than usual or are heavier than normal, then flooding almost always follows.

During February and March 2000, flooding in Southern Africa killed hundreds of people and left about 1.25 million homeless. Mozambique bore the brunt of the flooding, but Zimbabwe, Botswana, Zambia, and the island of Madagascar were also affected. The severe floods in Mozambique were caused by the extraordinary amount of rain that fell during February—45.6 inches (116 cm) compared with the average of 7 inches (17.7 cm). Rivers across the region burst their banks as Cyclone Eline swept in, bringing new rains to lands already waterlogged by more than two weeks of storms. Crops and village granaries were washed away, destroying food supplies, while roads, bridges, and dams were destroyed. Mozambique was cut in half by a strip of muddy water 31 miles (50 km) wide and up to 16.5 feet (5 m) deep. The flood left homes unfit to live in and drinking wells unusable. The floodwaters were contaminated by human sewage, and malarial mosquitoes bred in the pools of stagnant water.

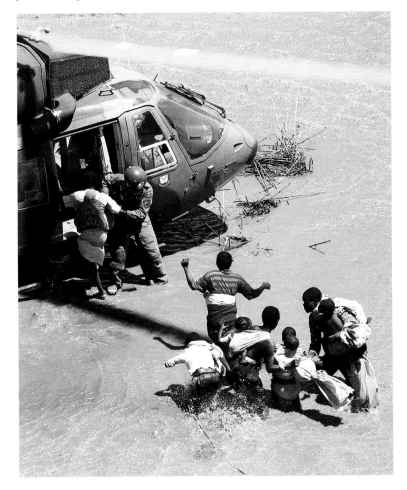

A helicopter belonging to the South African Army rescues flood victims from the banks of the Limpopo River in Mozambique.

Trees and flooding

In many parts of the world, wood is used for cooking, heating water, and keeping warm. Trees are cut down to clear land for crops and provide grazing land for animals. Without trees, the soil in which they grow is easily washed away. This is called deforestation.

In tropical climates, tree-covered slopes help to prevent flooding and mudslides. Forests on hillsides also keep fertile soils from washing away. In the rainy season, tree roots soak up much of the water as it sinks into the soil. If the trees did not act as living sponges, the water would fill streams and rivers and make them overflow. The tree roots also hold the soil together. When forests are cut or burned down, there is nothing to hold the soil in place, and it is washed away.

Storm surges and cyclones

Coastal floods can be caused by a storm surge. This sudden rise in sea level happens when water is piled up against the coast by strong winds blowing toward the land. The water may rise as much as 16.5 feet (5 m) above normal levels and cause widespread flooding and loss of life. Surges are common in the Gulf of Mexico, along the Atlantic coast of the U.S., around the islands of the western Pacific, and in the Bay of Bengal.

Bangladesh is often hit by cyclones. Only a quarter of the country lies more than 10 feet (3 m) above sea level, yet 117 million people live there. In April 1991, the surface of the sea off Bangladesh was whipped up by a tropical cyclone until it was 20 feet (6 m) higher than normal. This surge swept over low-lying areas of Bangladesh, killing 140,000 people and leaving millions more homeless. Six years later, another powerful tropical

A storm surge hits Western Samoa, a group of islands in the Pacific Ocean.

cyclone struck Bangladesh and damaged 400,000 homes. This time many lives were saved because better warnings had been given, and people took refuge in cyclone shelters built after the 1991 disaster.

The Yangtze River

The Yangtze is the longest river in China and the fourth-longest in the world. More than 700 small rivers join it on its 3,900-mile (6,300 km) journey across China, and nearly half of China's 1.2 billion people live near its banks. In 1998, exceptionally heavy rain caused the river to flood. The floods were worse than usual because over the years the trees on the slopes above the river had been cleared. The river banks gave way, hundreds of villages were destroyed, and millions of farmers were stranded on strips of higher ground. The flood affected 240 million people. About 3,000 were drowned, and millions more were left homeless.

Sinking cities

Many cities grew up around trading ports and lie close to sea level, which puts them at risk of flooding. Some are slowly sinking. In Bangkok, people take water from 10,000 wells under the city. As water is drawn from the wells, the rocks dry out and shrink, and the city sinks and is threatened by floods from the river and the Gulf of Thailand.

A similar disaster threatens the Italian city of Venice, by the Adriatic Sea. So much water has been taken from the ground that the city has sunk more than 4.5 inches (12 cm) in 50 years. At the same time, the sea has risen by about 3.5 inches (9 cm), and Venice now floods whenever there is a high tide combined with heavy rainfall and a storm surge.

Floods in the Piazza St. Marco, Venice, Italy. Because Venice is sinking, flooding is a common occurrence.

Floodwaters breaking through a levee built by the Mississippi River south of Quincy, Illinois, in 1993.

Protection from banks

A river carries huge quantities of mud and sand eroded from the sides and bottom as it flows from its source in the hills. In the lower course of a river, the water flows more slowly and drops mud and sand, raising the river bed. This happens with the Mississippi River in the U.S. As the river bed has risen, people nearby have built high banks, called levees, to keep the river from flooding their homes. In places, the levees are more than 20 feet (6 m) above the level of the Mississippi.

Dredging river beds

Dredgers can remove mud and sand from a river bed to deepen the river so that it holds more water. Some rivers meander from side to side in their lower parts. This slows down the flow of water and can cause flooding.

Straightening the channel so the water flows out to sea more quickly can prevent flooding, although it might make a river less suitable for plants and animals. Sometimes a relief channel is dug to divert floodwater away from the main river. Planting trees on steep slopes near rivers slows down the rate at which water flows down the slopes and into the river. It also helps to hold the soil in place so it is not washed into the river.

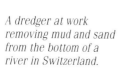

MISSISSIPPI FLOODS

The Mississippi River broke through its levees in 120 places in 1927. It flooded 26,000 square miles (67,000 sq km), 600,000 people lost their homes, and 246 people died.

A dredger at work removing mud and sand from the bottom of a river in Switzerland.

Dams and flood barriers

Some flooding can be prevented by dams or sluice gates. These hold back and store water in reservoirs and release it in a controlled way. There are disadvantages to constructing dams. The Aswan High Dam in Egypt holds back the waters of the Nile River in Lake Nasser and controls the flooding of hundreds of miles of the Nile valley to the north. The water from Lake Nasser irrigates large stretches of land and supplies hydroelectric power to Egypt's industries. However, vast quantities of the water in Lake Nasser evaporate in the heat of the sun, and much of the fertile mud that once spread over the fields during floods now clogs up the reservoir. The lake water is slightly salty, and when it evaporates, it builds up a layer of salt in the soil in which plants cannot grow. Now some areas of land downstream of the lake have become infertile.

Flood barriers are built across river mouths to protect towns and cities upstream from storm surges. To keep storm surges from the North Sea from flooding London, a barrier was built across the mouth of the River Thames. This is raised when surges and storm floods threaten.

The barrier built across the River Thames to stop storm surges from the North Sea from flooding London, England.

Coastal defenses

The best barriers against flooding from the sea are beaches, sand dunes, and salt marshes. These are all damaged by the growth of towns and resorts, and other human activities. Today, huge sums of money are spent on building artificial sea defenses. Sea walls of stone or concrete protect beaches and buildings. Most modern walls are curved to push the waves upward and back out to sea again.

Breakwaters are long barriers of boulders or concrete built into the sea. They protect harbors during stormy weather. However, they can sometimes redirect the damaging waves elsewhere. Groynes— fences on beaches at right angles to the sea—slow down water currents, preventing sand and pebbles from being washed away. In some places, artificial reefs—rows of rocks parallel to the coastline— are being built to reduce the power of the waves.

Soft engineering

Increasingly, people are using "soft engineering" techniques, such as planting marram grass, which is tolerant of salt, to prevent sand dunes from being blown away. Improving the drainage of soft cliffs can help to prevent cliff falls caused by heavy rain. Allowing seawater to flood coastal land can actually protect against flooding inland. Salt marshes provide a rich habitat for birds, wildfowl, plants, and other wildlife. Just as importantly, the marsh breaks the force of the waves, preventing flooding farther inland.

Landslides and mudslides

Somewhere in the world, a landslide is probably happening now. Landslides can be triggered by heavy rain, frost, melting snow, or an earthquake, causing huge masses of rock, soil, or mud to fall rapidly down a slope.

Ice and water

Many rocks are soft and porous, while others have many cracks in them. In cool, wet climates, the water that collects in these pores and cracks may later freeze. As the water freezes, it expands, and the ice presses against the sides of each pore or crack. On high mountains, water often freezes at night and melts again the next day. Eventually, the ice widens the cracks in the rock until pieces begin to break off. Rainwater is slightly acidic, and this acid slowly softens rocks such as chalk, limestone, and granite, so that pieces crumble away.

The effects of weathering

In hot, dry places, such as deserts, the heat during the day makes the rocks expand, while at night they cool and contract. This gradually weakens the rocks until pieces break off. Plant roots also break up rocks when they grow in cracks. As the roots grow, they force the sides of the crack farther apart, weakening the rock and splitting it. Burrowing animals can also widen cracks in rocks and weaken them.

Sometimes pieces of rock slide downhill as soon as they break off, forming scree, but usually the pieces collect in one place until something starts them moving. This can be a natural event such as heavy rain, melting snow, an earthquake, or waves from the sea. Human activities such as mining and quarrying can also set off a landslide.

A large bank of loose stones, called scree, at the bottom of a mountain in the Swiss Alps.

Rock slides

One of the most extreme kinds of rock fall happens when a mass of rock thunders down a slope. Sometimes a layer of air is trapped under the falling rock, which then floats along like a high-speed hovercraft. Rock slides of this kind are much more dangerous than simple rock falls because they often occur on the lower slopes of mountains, near farms and villages. Rock slides have killed many people and destroyed whole villages in the Canadian Rockies, Norway, Switzerland, and many other mountainous areas.

Mudslides

Mudslides form when soil or other loose material on a slope becomes soaked with water. This usually happens after a sudden, heavy rainstorm or when snow melts rapidly on hills and mountains. Some mudslides are caused by rainwater or melting snow mixing with the ash from a volcano. The wet material then no longer sticks to the slope, but slides downhill, flowing like a liquid.

In May 1998, heavy rain in the hills around Naples, Italy, washed thousands of tons of mud down into the valleys below. The mud came from hills where trees had been cut down or burned. The mud rushed down gullies like a tidal wave. It tore down houses and bridges and swept away cars and trees. Parts of some villages were buried under 6.5 feet (2 m) of mud. When the rain finally stopped, the sun baked the mud hard, making rescuers' work more difficult. At least 81 people were killed, and many more were injured.

Erupting volcanoes

Many volcanoes are so high that they are permanently covered in snow. If the volcano erupts, red-hot ash mixes with the melting snow and forms a very dangerous mudslide. This happened when the Nevado del Ruiz volcano in Colombia, South America, erupted in November 1995. The snow and ice on the volcano melted, and the water carried thousands of tons of ash as it rushed down the mountainside. One of the streams of mud was 132 feet (40 m) high, and some traveled 37 miles (60 km) before they finally came to a halt. Altogether, the mudslides killed more than 23,000 people and destroyed thousands of homes.

A large rock slide beside the Colorado River in Utah. Rock slides like this can be very dangerous if they happen near villages.

LARGEST LANDSLIDE

The world's largest landslide happened on the slopes of Mount St. Helens in Washington in May 1980. An earthquake triggered mudslides, landslides, and floods that released 99 billion cubic feet (2.8 billion cu m) of rock and mud. More than 100 square miles (259 sq km) of forest were destroyed, and about 10 people were killed, along with countless elk, deer, bears, and coyotes.

Drought

A drought is a long period of dry weather when no rain falls for weeks, months, or even years. Parts of the world that have a dry season and a wet season expect a drought every year. People plan for it by storing water and by growing crops that can withstand the dry weather. A drought is far worse when it is not expected.

The effects of drought

Droughts make lakes, rivers, reservoirs, and wells dry up because more water evaporates than falls as rain or snow. Plants wilt and die. Animals trample the ground as they search for food and water. If the drought is brief—a partial drought—many plants recover, and the damage is not lasting. If it is long, winds may blow away the topsoil and plants may catch fire. Most of them will not be able to regrow. If the rains fail in tropical areas, there is no water to store for the dry season. During a prolonged drought, with no crops for food, people starve unless they can find food elsewhere. In poorer parts of the world, droughts bring famine, disease, and huge numbers of deaths.

Catastrophic droughts

Droughts are more severe in some areas than in others. The worst droughts happen in areas bordering the deserts of the world. Where warm, tropical air masses descend north or south of the equator, they form an area of high pressure, or anticyclone, in hot desert areas. The clouds disperse, and rainfall is minimal. The drying out process is made worse by lots of sunshine and low humidity. If the prevailing winds shift from their normal path, then the high pressure, anticyclonic conditions of the permanently dry regions spread to areas that usually have a wet season and cause a drought.

The remains of a giraffe that died during a drought in Kenya. When plants wilt and die during a drought, plant-eating animals, or herbivores, quickly starve to death.

A southward shift of the prevailing westerly winds caused the most severe drought in the 20th century. This was in the Sahel, on the southern fringes of the Sahara Desert in Africa, which normally receives low rainfall. During the early 1960s, there was a series of good seasons, and many people settled on the edge of the desert. Then, at the end of the decade, a drought began that has continued on and off ever since. It was widespread in 1984 and 1985, when it caused crop failures and famine in 20 countries. Ethiopia had had low rainfall and poor harvests for years, made worse by a civil war from which millions of people had been forced to flee. About half a million people died there in 1985. Many scientists believe that the climate of the Sahara region is becoming drier as a result of long-term change. Over 10,000 years, once-fertile grasslands have become the largest hot desert in the world.

A tribesman searches for water in the desert in Ethiopia during a prolonged drought.

The dried-up Ladybower Reservoir in the Derwent Valley, South Yorkshire, England, during a drought.

Why the rains fail

Anything that interrupts the water cycle can produce a drought. Winds might change direction, taking rain-bearing clouds elsewhere. Sometimes an area of high pressure settles in one place for a long time. Then the air becomes very still and calm, and rain clouds cannot form, which leads to a serious drought. Droughts can also be caused by quite small changes in the temperature of the surface of the sea, or higher than average air temperatures. If the surface waters become warmer, there is less evaporation of water from the sea, so fewer clouds form.

Man-made drought

People create drought conditions by disrupting the water cycle. The Aral Sea, on the borders of Kazakhstan and Uzbekistan in Central Asia, was once the fourth largest inland sea in the world. It originally covered 26,250 square miles (68,000 sq km), but is now half that area, and more than 75 percent of its water has evaporated.

The sea was once a natural reservoir in a vast desert, and an important fishery. It began drying up in the 1960s, when people diverted the two rivers that flowed into it to use the water for irrigation. The irrigation ditches were poorly constructed, and the soil became waterlogged so that the crops of cotton and rice would not grow. Less water flowed into the Aral Sea, and the concentration of salt increased as water evaporated in the hot sun. This destroyed the fishing industry. Now, there are fishing villages 50 miles (80 km) from the water where fishing boats have been left high and dry.

A fishing boat marooned by the shrinking of the Aral Sea on the borders of Kazakhstan and Uzbekistan in Central Asia.

DRIEST PLACE

The world's driest place is the Atacama Desert in Chile. Rainfall there is barely measurable. Some places in the Atacama have had no rain for more than 400 years.

Sandstorms and dust storms

Sandstorms and dust storms happen during periods of drought. In desert areas, high winds lift sand particles into the air and blow a sandstorm across the landscape. This usually happens during the day, when the ground has become hot, and the storms die out at night as Earth cools down again. The force of the wind-blown sand can etch the glass of windows and sandpaper the paint from vehicles. Over a long period of time, sandstorms erode rocks into unusual shapes. The sand particles usually rise no more than 10 feet (3 m) above the ground, although occasionally they reach 50 feet (15 m). Millions of tons of sand can be shifted in just a few hours, and sand from the Sahara has even been blown to Britain and parts of South America.

A sandstorm in China. Over-intensive farming and climate change have caused deserts to spread in Asia and Africa, affecting millions of the world's poorest people.

Dust storms happen where farmland has been left bare or has dried out during a drought. Rising winds lift the loose, dusty soil and carry it for hundreds of miles. A dust storm can be up to 400 miles (640 km) wide and can lift the dust up to 14,000 feet (4,300 m).

During a dust storm, you cannot see more than 1,300 feet (400 m) ahead. The air is so thick with dust that no living thing can breathe. It blocks roads and railways; enters locked buildings, closed cupboards, food, and machines; and may hang in the air for days.

Wildfires

Plants become very dry during a drought, and wildfires often occur. Hot, dry winds fan the flames. Some wildfires are begun by lightning, but most are caused by people—usually by accident, but occasionally deliberately. Most fires started by lightning are eventually put out by rain. They may die out when they reach water or an area where there is little material to burn. If a wildfire is not controlled, it can rage across the countryside, causing widespread damage and loss of life. Fires also pollute the air with their smoke. In 1997 and 1998, Indonesia and Malaysia suffered their worst drought in 50 years. People used fires to clear areas of forest, but the monsoon rains did not come to put them out. The fires burned out of control for months, covering the area with smoke.

Wildfires, some caused by lightning and some started deliberately by people, are common during a drought. This wildfire is destroying eucalyptus woodland in Australia.

Useful fires

Although fires can damage property and crops, they can also be useful. Fires burn dried plants and dead wood and clear gaps in forests, where new tree seedlings can grow. After a fire in the dry African savanna grasslands, green shoots appear, providing food for grazing animals. Some plants, such as eucalyptus trees and banksia shrubs in Australia, rely on fire to release the seeds from their pods.

Eucalyptus trees sprout new growth three months after a wildfire in Australia.

The American Dust Bowl

Dry, dusty soil that is unprotected by plants easily blows away. The finest particles blow away first, leaving behind the less fertile larger particles. One of the most famous examples of this occurred in the Great Plains in the U.S. During the 1860s, several rainy years transformed this area, which had previously been very dry. The few farmers who had settled there enjoyed good harvests until 1887, when drought struck again.

During the early 20th century, the rains brought good harvests again. In the 1920s, people who had little knowledge of how to farm fragile soils settled on large areas of the natural prairie grassland there. Millions of acres of grassland in Colorado, New Mexico, Texas, and Oklahoma were plowed and planted with grain crops. The shallow roots of these plants could not bind the soil, whereas the interlocking roots of the natural grasses formed a mat of roots just below the surface, which held the fine soil in place. To increase profits, the farmers grew the same grain crops year after year, rather than allowing the soil to rest (lie fallow) some years. They also raised cattle, which overgrazed the soil. Eventually, the overworked soil became dry

PEOPLE AND DESERTS

The United Nations calculates that more than 250 million people suffer from the results of desertification— the spreading of desert conditions— while a billion more are at risk.

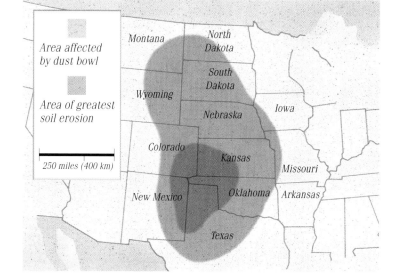

THE NORTH AMERICAN DUST BOWL
This map shows the huge area of farmland affected by drought during the 1930s in the Great Plains.

Area affected by dust bowl

Area of greatest soil erosion

250 miles (400 km)

Montana · North Dakota · South Dakota · Wyoming · Nebraska · Iowa · Colorado · Kansas · Missouri · New Mexico · Oklahoma · Arkansas · Texas

A small-scale irrigation project in the Sinai Desert in Egypt. Used carefully, irrigation helps farmers grow good crops in desert soils.

and powdery. In 1932, the Great Plains region suffered a severe drought. Vast areas had low rainfall for almost a decade, and for five years there was no rain. Crops failed, and fierce storms and hot, dry winds blew away the dry topsoil in swirling clouds.

One gale in 1934 swept across the U.S. and picked up more than 385,800 tons (350,000 t) of the dusty soil. Birds suffocated in midair, and cities such as New York were plunged into darkness when clouds of dust blotted out the sun. Thousands of farmers were ruined, and more than 350,000 people had to abandon their homes. Thousands more died of starvation or of lung diseases caused by breathing in the dust-laden air. Relief finally arrived in 1940, when there was heavy rainfall across the region. After similar rainfalls in 1941, the disaster was over, but fewer than half of the farmers were left in the region.

Improved farming methods

In 1935, the American government began to improve what had become known as the Dust Bowl. Some land was planted with grasses to bind the soil. Crops were planted in rotation so that they did not damage the soil, and fields were rested every third year. Hedges and windbreaks of trees were planted to lessen the force of the wind. Reservoirs were built to store water. Despite this, every 10 years or so, there have been droughts and destructive dust storms when the soils remain vulnerable. In Russia, too, dry areas of the steppes were plowed and planted with grain crops after World War II, and similar severe dust bowl erosion occurred.

Modern drought precautions

Drought cannot be predicted reliably, but there are precautions that can be taken if the money is available to pay for them. Reservoirs can be built to store water when it does rain, and irrigation channels can be dug to carry this water to crops. Terraces can be cut into sloping fields, or ridges of stone can be laid across them, to prevent rainwater from running away down slopes.

Drought-resistant trees, such as acacias and eucalyptus trees, can be planted as windbreaks and to keep soil from blowing away. Crops grow strongly in the shade of the trees, which eventually provide valuable firewood. Putting animal manure and compost on dry soil helps it hold water longer. These materials also bind the soil particles together and prevent them from blowing away. Farmers can learn about the dangers of overcropping and overgrazing, and governments can try to keep people from settling in drought-prone areas.

Ice and snow

8

A landscape blanketed by pristine white snow is
a beautiful sight. Plants with a sparkling coat of frost
can look equally attractive. But ice and snow can bring
traffic to a standstill and can be deadly to people.

Blizzards

A combination of heavy snowfall, low temperatures, and strong winds
creates a blizzard. A snow storm is called a blizzard if the wind speed is
greater than 35 miles (56 km) per hour. A blizzard can bring whole cities to
a standstill. In addition to disrupting transportation, it brings down power
lines, leaving whole communities without electricity. A blizzard that
dumped 47 inches (120 cm) of snow on the east coast of the U.S. in
February 2003 left more than 225,000 people without electricity. People
with no other means of heating or cooking begin to suffer from
hypothermia. Those at greatest risk are babies and elderly people.

The storm of the century

North America suffered a blizzard that earned the title of the storm of the
century in March 1993. Satellite images showed a huge mass of cold air
moving down from the north polar regions. When it reached the Gulf of
Mexico, it collided violently with warm, moist air in the region.

*New Yorkers struggle
through a snowstorm
on foot.*

The storm that resulted swept across Cuba, bringing torrential rain, hurricane-force winds, and mountainous waves. About 1,500 houses were destroyed and 37,000 badly damaged.

The storm then turned north and grew colder. Florida was battered by fierce winds and unusually heavy snowfall. The blizzard moved up the southeastern side of the U.S., powered by winds of up to 125 miles (200 km) per hour. Heavy snowfall collapsed roofs and brought down power lines. In the state of North Carolina, storm surges wrecked beachfront houses, and 60 inches (152 cm) of snow fell on the Appalachian Mountains.

In the northern U.S. and Canada, people were better prepared. But 10 inches (25 cm) of snow brought New York City to a standstill, and the major airports in the eastern U.S. were closed. The 1993 blizzard was responsible for 243 deaths and caused $3 billion in damage. This would have been much worse had weather forecasters not been able to give early warning of the storm's arrival.

Large parts of the U.S. were again brought to a standstill by a blizzard in January 1996. The state of Philadelphia was buried under more than 30 inches (76 cm) of snow, while New York received at least 20 inches (51 cm), and 23 people died. A blizzard on New Year's Eve in 2000 blanketed New York and New Jersey with 16 inches (40 cm) of snow, bringing widespread disruption.

WET OR DRY SNOW?

As a general rule, 10 inches (25 cm) of snow produces the same amount of water as 1 inch (2.5 cm) of rain. But different types of snow vary. When snow is very dry and powdery at low temperatures, 30 inches (76 cm) is equivalent to 1 inch (2.5 cm) of rain. When snow is soft and wet and falls at a temperature just above the freezing point, as little as four inches (10 cm) of snow is equivalent to one inch (2.5 cm) of rain.

Mediterranean blizzards

From time to time, blizzards affect countries bordering the Mediterranean Sea. In February 2004, blizzards cut off 2,700 villages in Turkey. Two ships sank off the Turkish coast near Istanbul, with the loss of 20 lives. The neighboring countries of Bulgaria and Greece were also badly affected, and 20 inches (51 cm) of snow fell on the Greek capital, Athens.

Ice storms

Ice storms are formed when rain that has fallen through warmer air meets a layer of very cold air near the ground. The rain does not have time to change to sleet. Instead, it turns to ice when it touches any solid object.

In January 1998, a severe ice storm lasting five days raged through eastern Canada and the northeastern U.S. More than 220,000 people lost power in Maine alone. The ice destroyed 2,500 power poles and brought down thousands of miles of power lines. Falling trees and icy roads made travel impossible. In eastern Canada, the storm brought down 80,150 miles (129,000 km) of power lines along with 1,000 power poles, leaving 3 million people without power.

Frozen vegetation after an ice storm in Central Oklahoma.

How avalanches are caused

The most dramatic killer in cold climates is the avalanche. A huge mass of snow, usually mixed with ice, soil, and rock, rushes down a mountain destroying everything in its path. An avalanche creates a strong wind on either side that can be powerful enough to uproot trees.

Avalanches begin high on mountains above the snow line, where temperatures are below freezing, so that fresh falls of snow pile up, rather than melting. As more and more snow accumulates, its weight turns the lower layers into ice, which begins to slide down the mountainside. On steep slopes, the ice layer can be eroded by spring rains or a rise in temperature as the winter snows begin to melt. A sudden, heavy fall of snow that does not have time to stick to the rock, ice, or snow beneath it can also set off an avalanche.

An avalanche sliding down a mountainside can be extremely powerful and can reach speeds of 200 miles (320 km) per hour. Avalanches can kill people even inside their homes. This happened to the inhabitants of the village of Ozengeli in Turkey when an avalanche hit in January 1993. Rescuers dug out 21 survivors, but 53 people died.

During the winter of 1999, the Austrian Alps had mild weather followed by heavy snowfalls and strong winds. A block of snow, probably weighing 187,000 tons (170,000 t), broke away from the side of a mountain and crashed onto the village of Galtur below. More than 30 people were killed.

Types of avalanches

There are two main kinds of avalanches. In very cold, dry weather, light powdery snow grains do not stick together. If this type of snow starts to move down the mountain, it forms a

A massive avalanche crashes down a mountain near the ski resort of Telluride in southwest Colorado.

INSIDE AN AVALANCHE

To study avalanches from the inside, scientists in Montana have built an underground lookout post on a mountain slope. With the help of explosives, they set off an avalanche. As it rushes down the mountain, the avalanche passes over the lookout, from where the scientists film and study it. One of their findings is that the temperature of the avalanche materials increases as it slides down the mountain. The farther the avalanche has traveled, the greater the increase. The aim of the research is to learn how to forecast avalanches accurately.

powder avalanche that swirls along like a huge, white cloud. A slab avalanche is more dangerous, and it starts off as a solid chunk of frozen snow about the size of a football field and about 30 feet (9 m) deep. This sort of avalanche often forms when sunny days are followed by frosty nights, causing melted snow to freeze again.

Limiting the damage

Every year, about 100 million people visit the European Alps. Avalanches kill about 150 of them. In the U.S., avalanches have killed more than 500 people since 1950. As more people enjoy winter sports in the mountains, the need to anticipate avalanches is growing. Trained snow patrols carry out "snow profiles" to predict avalanches. By looking closely at the snow layers and their temperatures, guides can estimate how stable the packed snow is. When snow and ice are precariously balanced, even a small vibration can trigger an avalanche. A sudden gust of wind or a noise such as a loud shout or thunder can set one off. When an avalanche threatens, explosives or rockets can be used to bring it down. A small, planned avalanche is easier to deal with than a large, unexpected one. At the slightest danger, warnings are broadcast, and roads and ski hills are closed.

FRESH SNOW

The risk of an avalanche is greatest when fresh, loose snow falls on a layer of frozen snow. The slightest disturbance will cause a huge block of newly fallen snow to slide into the valley below.

This concrete tunnel protects a road from avalanches in central Switzerland.

These metal fences are designed to break up any avalanche forming on the slopes of this mountain in Mannlichen, Switzerland.

El Niño

9

Oceans have a major effect on weather and climate, and none more so than the Pacific. Here, a current of warm water in the Pacific Ocean that usually flows east changes direction every two to seven years. This causes extreme climate changes in some parts of the world.

DROUGHTS

The growth of the world's deserts and the long drought in Africa's Sahel region have been blamed on global warming. Scientists now believe these events were partly due to El Niño.

Normal El Niño

In a normal year, trade winds blow from east to west across the equatorial part of the Pacific Ocean and push water warmed by the tropical sun west. The waters on the western side of the Pacific may be more than 18 °F (10 °C) warmer than on the eastern side. Over the warm water, the air pressure is low, and lighter, moist air rises to bring clouds and heavy rain to Southeast Asia, New Guinea, and northern Australia. On the eastern side of the Pacific, where the seawater is cold, air pressure is high. Few clouds form, so there is little rain along the western coasts of South America. When an El Niño event occurs, and the current flows farther south, the cold area in the eastern Pacific and the warm western area swap. The pressure reverses, and the trade winds weaken or reverse direction. The warm water moves east along the equator toward the South American coast, where it spreads north and south. On the western side of the Pacific, no rain falls, and there is drought. India, the Sahel, southern Africa and Brazil also have drought.

NORMAL OCEAN CURRENTS

In a normal year, trade winds blow from east to west across the Pacific Ocean. Water warmed by the tropical sun is pushed west. On the eastern side of the Pacific, the seawater is cold.

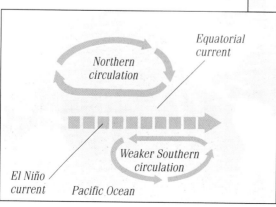

Northern circulation

Equatorial current

Southern circulation

Pacific Ocean

Northern circulation

Equatorial current

El Niño current

Weaker Southern circulation

Pacific Ocean

EL NIÑO CURRENTS

During an El Niño event, the current flows farther south. The cold area and warm area of the Pacific Ocean swap places, and the trade winds weaken or reverse direction.

Floods and typhoons

El Niño has effects worldwide because changes in ocean temperature bring about changes in the atmosphere. The warm surface water heats the air above, encouraging storms, typhoons, and hurricanes. There are droughts in some parts of the world, and increased rain in others, with floods and mudslides in northern Peru, Ecuador, and California. At the same time, the northern U.S. has a warmer and drier winter than usual.

El Niño also affects fisheries and wildlife along the coast of South America. Here, cold waters rich in nutrients well up from the bottom of the Pacific along the coast. The nutrients provide food for plankton, which in turn feed fish and other wildlife. In an El Niño year, the warm surface water along the coast of South America prevents the nutrient-rich water from rising to the surface. There is less food for the fish, which die or migrate to colder waters in search of food.

La Niña

An El Niño event is often followed by a period of unusual cooling in the tropical eastern side of the Pacific Ocean. This is called La Niña, and its effects are the opposite of El Niño's, although just as extreme. Extra-strong winds push more warm surface water than usual west toward Indonesia. Around the Americas, cold, deep seawater rises to fill the space. Less evaporation takes place, so rainfall and storms are less frequent in the east but more frequent over the warm waters of the western Pacific.

Corals are especially sensitive to the temperature of seawater. This coral has been bleached (and killed) by the warming of the Indian Ocean around the Maldive islands.

What's behind El Niño events?

No one really knows what makes El Niño sometimes behave differently. Some scientists believe that global warming is the cause. Other scientists argue that the phenomenon has been around for thousands of years, so could not be caused by recent global warning. There are many conflicting opinions about this: Some scientists believe that there is no such thing as La Niña, and that the weather at this time is just normal.

Recent El Niño reverses began in 1984, 1991, 1994, 1997, and 2003. The effects of the changed pattern can last for up to four years. The El Niño event of 1997 was the most extreme of the 20th century. Indonesia and other parts of Southeast Asia suffered the worst drought in 50 years, followed by massive forest fires. Australia also suffered severe drought and bushfires.

A chain of buoys now stetches across nearly one-third of the world in the tropical Pacific. The buoys collect information on ocean temperature and winds, which is fed into computers to help scientists give early warnings of an El Niño event. Perhaps they may eventually also help to explain this complex and potentially devastating weather pattern.

Glossary

air pressure The force of the air pressing down on Earth's surface.

anticyclone A large area of high pressure (sometimes called a high) from which all winds blow outward.

atmosphere The blanket of gases around a planet, held there by the pull of the planet's gravity.

avalanche A rapid movement of snow, sometimes combined with ice and rock material, down a steep slope.

barometer An instrument for measuring air pressure.

blizzard Severe weather conditions that combine heavy snow, strong winds, low temperatures, and poor visibility.

climate The average weather in a place over a long period of time.

clouds Masses of water droplets or ice particles floating in the atmosphere. There are 10 types, with 3 basic groups: stratus, cumulus, and cirrus.

condensation The process by which a vapor or gas changes into a liquid as it cools.

current A body of air or water moving in a definite direction.

cyclone (see hurricane)

deforestation The permanent removal of forests.

depression An area of low pressure, sometimes called a low, which brings unsettled weather. It may also be called a cyclone.

dew point The temperature at which water vapor in the air condenses.

doldrums A belt of calm or very light winds, but with occasional sudden storms, near the equator.

drizzle Light rain that is made of drops that are less than 0.02 inches (0.5 mm) in diameter.

drought A long period of dry weather, with no rainfall.

evaporation The process by which a liquid is changed into a vapor or gas when it is heated.

fog A cloud that has come down to ground level and that has reduced visibility to less than a half-mile (1 km).

forecast (weather)
A statement of how the weather is likely to change in the future in a particular place.

frost White ice crystals that form on cold surfaces when moisture from the air freezes.

global warming The warming of Earth's atmosphere due to air pollution.

greenhouse effect
The warming of Earth, caused by certain gases in the atmosphere, called greenhouse gases. These allow the sun's rays to reach Earth's surface but trap heat given off by the ground.

hail Rounded pellets of ice that fall from cumulonimbus clouds.

humidity The amount of water vapor present in the air.

hurricane A violent tropical storm in the Caribbean and North Atlantic with winds blowing at 75 miles (120 km) per hour or more around a low pressure center. It is known as a typhoon in the northwestern Pacific and a cyclone in the Indian Ocean and around Australia.

ice age One of several periods in Earth's history when huge glaciers and ice sheets covered large parts of the land surface.

ice storm A storm in which falling rain freezes as soon as it touches any object on Earth's surface that is below the freezing point.

meteorology The study of how the atmosphere creates the weather and climate.

mist A cloud resting on the ground or sea that reduces visibility to 0.5 to 1.25 miles (1–2 km).

monsoon A wind that blows from different directions at different times of the year, causing wet and dry seasons, particularly in southern Asia, northern Australia, and western Africa.

polar front The boundary (or front) between warm tropical air and cold polar air in the middle latitudes north and south of the equator. Frontal depressions form and travel along it.

precipitation Any form of water (solid or liquid) that falls from the atmosphere and reaches the ground.

prevailing wind The main direction from which the wind blows in particular places.

rain shadow An area of decreased rainfall on the lee, or sheltered, side of a hill or mountain.

relative humidity The ratio between the actual amount of water vapor in the air and the maximum amount it can hold at a given temperature.

relief rainfall Rainfall resulting from hills and mountains causing clouds to rise and cool.

satellite A moon or spacecraft that moves in an orbit around a planet.

sleet A mixture of snow and rain, or partially melted snow.

snow line The lowest level on a mountain above which snow never completely disappears.

stratosphere The layer of the atmosphere that lies above the troposphere.

temperature A measure of how hot or cold something is.

timberline The upper limit of tree growth on a mountain.

tornado An intense, rotating column of air, shaped like a funnel, column, or rope, that extends downward from the base of a cloud to the ground.

trade wind Steady winds in the tropics blowing from the northeast in the northern hemisphere and from the southeast in the southern hemisphere.

troposphere The layer of the atmosphere that lies closest to Earth. This is where our weather occurs.

typhoon (see hurricane)

vacuum A completely empty space; a space without any air in it.

water cycle The continuous circulation of water from Earth's surface to the atmosphere, involving evaporation, condensation, and precipitation.

waterspout A rotating column of air that extends downward from the base of a cloud to touch a water surface. It is usually less violent than a tornado.

water vapor Water in the form of an invisible gas.

weather What is happening in the atmosphere at any particular time and place in terms of clouds, humidity, sunshine, temperature, visibility, precipitation, air pressure, and wind.

wind chill The sensation that the air temperature is lower than it really is because of the cooling effect of the wind on the human body.

Index